More praise for *Zentivity*:

"Marianne Clyde's *Zentivity* provides a fresh look at a serious and growing problem in the workforce: stress. Her innovative and simple tools for addressing stress and emotional triggers get right to the core of an issue. I tried one of the exercises and in an instant, I released an old belief that I hadn't even realized was active. I felt great. Anything that helps us gain balance and calm and to communicate effectively is a tremendous asset. I encourage everyone in business to use these tools. They work!"

—Shari J. Goodwin,
Business and Leadership Coach, Founder, Jaeger2

"Marianne Clyde has written a book with so much insight, support, and guidance to us on so many levels. This book really resonates with my 30+ years of working in health and human services, specifically in the field of addictions and mental health services. I thoroughly enjoyed and highly recommend to all, especially my colleagues, and their colleagues, as well as those who love us. One can only gain from reading this book; Marianne taps into the reality of our lives, personally and professionally—after all, these are all intersecting working relationships. *Zentivity* is the goal, destination, and the journey we crave and aim for!"

—Carolyn Castro-Donlan,
Ph.D., Founder, Owner, and CEO at
Castro-Donlan Consulting, LLC and
Imagine A Holistic Approach, LLC

"*Zentivity* captures precisely what modern society needs to get back to the basics and create a healthy and sustainable balance between personal life and work. The 10 principles are a strong foundation to accompany the illustrated strategies that will lead to a work environment where all succeed and thrive."

—Kumi Sato,
President and CEO, COSMO
Public Relations Corporation, Tokyo

"*Zentivity* is an inspiring new way to look at what could be holding us down—and innovative ways to get out of that paradigm into a world full of possibilities and positivity. Easy-to-follow advice about important life skills is interspersed with hard-to-forget stories that helped me visualize what *Zentivity* living can be.

—Geeta Mehta,
Adjunct Professor of Architecture and Urban Design at Columbia University in New York, Founder and President of Asia Initiatives

"Marianne Clyde has put together a clear picture of the modern work life and its stresses that tear at the fabric of our work places. The tools she shares to achieve *Zentivity* are fantastic, practical methods to help both employees and employers find balance, and improve their lives and productivity."

—Lantie Elisabeth Jorandby, M.D.,
General and Addiction Psychiatrist, Amen Clinics Inc. DC

"Intellect, technical skills, or business plans mean nothing without a healthy team of employees to execute. *Zentivity* outlines a succinct yet impactful strategy to bringing humanity back into the workplace for optimal performance. Bravo for hitting the elephant on the head."

—Chris Schembra,
Founder and Chief Question Asker, 7:47 Club

Zentivity

How to Eliminate Chaos, Stress, and Discontent in Your Workplace

Marianne Clyde

BALBOA
PRESS

A DIVISION OF HAY HOUSE

Balboa Press books may be ordered through booksellers or by contacting:

Balboa Press
A Division of Hay House
1663 Liberty Drive
Bloomington, IN 47403
www.balboapress.com
1 (877) 407-4847

Because of the dynamic nature of the internet, any web addresses or links contained in this book may have changed since publication and may no longer be valid. The views expressed in this work are solely those of the author and do not necessarily reflect the views of the publisher, and the publisher hereby disclaims any responsibility for them.

The author of this book does not dispense medical advice or prescribe the use of any technique as a form of treatment for physical, emotional, or medical problems without the advice of a physician, either directly or indirectly. The intent of the author is only to offer information of a general nature to help you in your quest for emotional and spiritual well-being. In the event you use any of the information in this book for yourself, which is your constitutional right, the author and the publisher assume no responsibility for your actions.

Print information available on the last page.

ISBN: 978-1-5043-8302-8 (sc)
ISBN: 978-1-5043-8304-2 (hc)
ISBN: 978-1-5043-8303-5 (e)

Library of Congress Control Number: 2017910079

Balboa Press rev. date: 07/06/2017

CONTENTS

Other books by Marianne Clyde

Peaceful Parenting: 10 Essential Principles (2013)

*Un-Leashed: Practical Steps to Get
Your Life Unstuck (2016)*

Dedication

To all the hardworking leaders out there who are spinning too many plates and feeling overwhelmed with all their responsibilities, while trying to create the life of their dreams. To you, I say, just breathe. You've got this!

FOREWORD

I first met Marianne in Tokyo close to two decades ago. She is one of those rare people with magical stardust that she generously sprinkles, transforming those it touches. People start to believe they have the power to achieve what they truly want. Her manner is calm and peaceful, yet underneath is an energy that she shares selflessly, helping people take real action to get to where they need to be.

We all read great books on how to move forward, but often that is just what we do—read them. What is different with Marianne is she wants to enable everyone to help themselves to the life they want to live. She wants them to act. She wants to empower them and give them the tools to take action. This book is practical. It describes how we all need to form our own very personal "locus of control" and demonstrates it with real examples that bring the subject to life.

The aptly named *Zentivity* focuses mainly on the workplace. The real issue Marianne challenges us on is how to authentically eliminate discontent in our workplace. It gives examples of how not to be continually knocked off our stride by negative, external personal or professional events we cannot control. We are not the victims.

When we have our personal locus of control, we choose to own who we are and what we stand for. This is not an aggressive stance; this is who we are, and we are living the life we were born to lead.

This allows us to be more effective leaders, employees, and parents. On a business front, there is nothing more rewarding for employers, customers, shareholders, and of course ourselves. The happiest days of my career have always been when I am so engaged with what I am working on that I forget to eat.

Zentivity is a foundation to any other business book. If you don't have that strong internal locus of control to keep you centered, balanced, and unaffected by external circumstances, you will continue to spin your wheels and run in too many directions, sapping your energy and causing you to continue to self-sabotage, no matter how many other books you read or courses you take.

Of course, this is all easier said than done, and we all have those competing pressures of personal and professional issues. We are not machines; they do spill over. This is where Marianne comes to the forefront and helps us work through it. I know of no one better qualified than Marianne to help provide the building blocks to allow us to gift the above to ourselves.

Marianne's life work has been in this field, both academically and practically. She has many years of experience traveling to developing countries, dealing with a myriad of diverse people who have experienced trauma. She teaches emotional healing and personal empowerment. Again, the principles are the same, whether you are rebuilding your country or family, or increasing employee engagement. She shows us how to own that space and lets us into her world. She uses real life issues, transforming this from theoretical suggestions to an actual playbook.

The book provides real insights, some of them you may find obvious, on how to live a more abundant life at work and outside. The key is to actually live them.

There were many lessons in the book that sounded a klaxon of common sense in my head. I try to practice them all. *Zentivity* gave more for me to reflect on and develop the discipline to have a behavioral change.

I found the lesson of Acceptance and being aware that curve balls will come is key. Do not be shocked when this happens: look forward to them to test yourself. Accept that this is part of life.

I have seen many millennials with tattoos saying Breathe in various languages, and I agree. This helps me not only to recover my IQ when stressed, but it buys me time before I answer.

I have lived in Asia since the late 1990s, and the idea of stepping outside of your body is something I do regularly. I even invented an imaginary little box to put all my negative thoughts into so I can Detach from the issue (or person) at hand to give me more objectivity. Often the negative thought just dissolves in the imaginary box and goes away, but if it doesn't, it can be revisited at a better time.

Clarity is one of the most important qualities in a leader, so everyone knows your expectations. Many great leaders are introverts, but they still have the responsibility to communicate clearly. Everyone wants to understand the plan and their part in the mission.

The last is always Respect. You can say almost anything as long as it is done with respect.

My family and I have been blessed to live in almost all corners of the world over the last thirty years, from the more developing and exciting African markets to Hong Kong, where we reside today. I have made many mistakes and would have loved to have a copy of *Zentivity* by my side all those years ago. Today is a great time to be alive in the business world as we disrupt and hopefully improve the business models of the past.

Marianne has written a powerful book that is a privilege to have and should be on everyone's desk as a reference guide, not just to be read once. Those that can execute what is proposed will draw up their own plans for a life of meaning and will probably find some of Marianne's stardust in their pocket.

Gordon T. Watson
Chair, Shared Value Project, Hong Kong
Regional Chief Executive, AIA Group

ACKNOWLEDGEMENTS

I would be remiss if I did not take this chance to thank the incredible executives, business owners, and managers who took the time to answer my questions and give me their valuable insights into what is important to them and their feedback on what works in their businesses. It's such a delight to hear how things got better for them when they implemented the principles of Zentivity.

Thanks also to Judy Olsen, owner of Judy Olsen Designs, for the lovely book cover and to Nancy Griffin-Bonnaire of Mark My Words, Inc., for putting in so many hours of editing to make things just right.

Zentivity

A peaceful, calm environment in which employees are actively engaged in the creative and productive process, taking ownership in the process and results of their work. End result: Companies make more money due to better employee retention and cooperation.

INTRODUCTION

Are You Ready for the Unexpected?

Sandra was leading a fast-paced, synergistic sales meeting. Everyone was involved in the discussion. Goals had been more than met for the year, so they were dreaming big! Hopes and spirits were high. Sandra was a great sales manager: positive, encouraging, enthusiastic, and a stellar example of what is possible when you put your mind to a task and stay focused.

She noticed in the back of the room that her assistant was signaling that she had an urgent phone call, so she excused herself, encouraging the brainstorming to continue and assuring the team that she'd be right back.

She picked up the phone, not recognizing the number, wondering what could be so important.

She stood frozen while the male voice on the other end prattled on endlessly, not making any sense at all. How could this be? Her husband would never do that. "This is crazy," she said. "You must have the wrong number."

"Is this Sandra Rollins?" he asked.

"Yes, and I am really sorry to hear that your wife is having an affair, but I don't know what that has to do with me."

"Didn't you get the photos I texted you?"

"Of course not, I am in the middle of a meeting. Who is this?"

Her head was spinning; it was difficult to switch gears so quickly. And what this guy was saying didn't make any sense at all. Her husband and this guy's wife? Having an affair? How could that be? But as she glanced at the texts that she had been ignoring and saw picture after picture of her husband with a young woman, obviously more than just friends, she felt nausea rising in her stomach.

"What are you saying?" she demanded of the guy on the other end of the phone.

"I am saying that your husband and my wife are having an affair, and I thought you should know. That's all. It's been going on for at least a year…" His voice trailed off. She couldn't focus any more. She. Had. To. Think. She couldn't breathe. She had to get out of there.

Sandra brushed by her shocked assistant, mumbling something about having to take care of something and instructing her to "let Jim wrap up the meeting," and ran out the door.

She tried to call her husband. No answer. Texted him. No response. Called him again and again. She drove home on autopilot, crashed through the door, pushed her dog out of the way, and poured a shot of whiskey to calm her trembling hands. And another, because the first didn't work.

By the time her husband walked through the door that evening, she was almost incoherent. "Why didn't you answer my calls, you bastard?" she attacked. And so it began. The confrontation, the tears, the denial, the proof, the yelling, the name-calling, and the drinking. They battled for hours until she was so exhausted that she collapsed on the couch and her husband stormed out.

The next morning, Sandra was groggy, devastated, and hung over. She looked in the mirror. "I can't go to work looking like this," she said, so she called in sick. She dragged her body into bed, where she stayed for the rest of the day.

Her kids got themselves ready for school, tip-toeing around whispering, "What's wrong with Mom?"

"I don't know; hurry, or we'll miss the bus."

She was still in bed when her kids and husband came home, and the scene from the night before replayed itself. He stormed out; she stayed in bed for three more days, unable to process what was happening and incapable of doing anything about it. The kids figured things out and did what they had to do, but started acting out in school.

She put off calls from the office. She knew decisions had to be made about work, but nothing seemed to interest her in the least.

One thing led to another. The marriage was in shambles; the kids were frightened and uneasy. The office sales team, who were compassionate at first, became annoyed. And it may not surprise you that Sandra was so shaken up that her productivity level went down, and the company appointed a new sales manager.

How did we ever get the idea that our personal lives don't impact our work? If problems are not tended to up front, they compound and overflow into every area of our lives: our physical health and well-being, our personal relationships and jobs, and ultimately the company's bottom line.

When we apply for a job, we are convinced that we can keep everything separate. Many of our bosses expect that as well. "I can't be bothered with their personal problems; I have a company to run!" they say.

That may be so, but what I have found from talking to business owners whom I know and trust, it seems that we must find ways to help our employees deal with their personal lives in a productive and compassionate way so the company that you "need to run" doesn't get run into the ground.

This is not a book about business strategy or how to write a business plan. It's not about strategic planning or corporate social responsibility. It's a book about human frailties and emotions. Whether or not you want to believe it, these things *do* find their way into the workplace and affect employee happiness and productivity. And workplace stresses find their way into the home, too.

If you are human, you have feelings. If you are human, you are in some kind of a relationship with someone. If you are human, you have certain needs, desires, and expectations about how things should be done. And what makes us interesting is that none of us thinks exactly alike or responds the same way to every situation. And herein lies the rub.

Every day for many years, I have worked with people to whom life has thrown a curve ball. When something unexpected crashes into our neatly planned lives and disrupts the status quo, we panic. And when we panic, we react.

Believe it or not, when we react out of a strong negative emotion like anger, hurt, or fear, adrenalin and cortisol are released, and our IQ actually goes down. We are immediately thrown into fight or flight mode, causing our actions to become instinctive and reactive to the information thrown at us, instead of being thoughtfully and mindfully received and answered with a wisely executed response.

A few things have become apparent to me. First, people react from the information that is already planted in their brains. From my experience, I would say that 90–95% of our reactions to adult problems stem from beliefs that we formed in childhood and have never fully examined. When we are children, our brains absorb information and feelings as truth, and we often develop a belief system that says, "I am defective." "I am not loveable." "I don't matter." And when reality intervenes and doesn't fit into our paradigm, we become defensive and reactive. We respond with a child's coping mechanism, which may have worked at one time, but it no longer serves us. This needs to change.

Second, because of these beliefs that we view as truth, we don't have a strong foundation on which to build. So we keep building on a foundation that says, "I am not worthy," or "I am not capable." No wonder our worlds seem to crumble around us. We need to re-examine our internal conversations that lurk below the surface of our consciousness, changing the beliefs to help us develop a firm foundation. This way, when the winds of trouble or misfortune blow hard against us, we can stand strong and calmly find the solution that is always present—if we know where to look.

Until we do these things, we will carry our burdens from our home life into our work and drag the heaviness from conflicts at work back home. Our energy will be depleted. Stress will continue to bring instability and disease into our lives, robbing us of the rewards that we have worked so hard for, limiting our ability to be creative and productive, and stealing the joy that comes from a life well-lived.

In the pages that follow, I will guide you to find a calm, quiet, secure mindset that you will be able to achieve both at home and in the office. Once you learn how to carry that with you, you'll wonder how you've survived thus far without it.

Throughout this book, you will learn how to be aware of your environment and your reaction to it. I'll discuss how to recognize emotions and what's really triggering them. We'll examine beliefs, and if they are working against us, we'll change them. I'll explain what healthy communication looks and feels like, and you'll find that all the tools in this book glean better results than our old knee-jerk reactions.

You will hear from business owners and executives about what it's like on the front lines: what has and hasn't worked for them, and you'll incorporate all that information into a package to help you find freedom from traps that keep you stuck, both personally and professionally. I'll offer solutions and suggestions for raising your satisfaction levels in your personal life and your business life, noticing where one bleeds into the other and how to minimize the damage at home and at work.

PART ONE
Things that Keep Us Stuck

Most of our unhappiness
comes from our refusal to
let something go.
Release it. Forgive. Say
goodbye.
Choose joy.
It's good for your health.

Marianne Clyde

CHAPTER 1

Raising Awareness

Here are the facts:

Approximately one million U.S. employees miss work each day due to workplace stress. (*Health Advocate, Inc.* 2009)

Job stress carries a price tag for U.S. industry estimated at over $300 billion annually as a result of absenteeism, employee turnover, diminished productivity, and other workplace related expenses. (American Institute of Stress)

Unscheduled absenteeism costs roughly $3,600 per year for each hourly worker and $2,650 per year for salaried employees. (*Forbes*, July 10, 2013)

Eighty percent of workers feel stress on the job; nearly half say they need help in learning how to manage stress; and 42% say their coworkers need such help. (American Institute of Stress, August 2011)

With 65% of U.S. employees citing work as a significant source of stress and more than one-third reporting chronic work stress, workplace stress can affect both individual well-being and organizational performance. (American Psychological Association, 2016)

Fifty-one percent of workers say that they are less productive at work because of stress. (American Psychological Association, 2009)

A study by economists at the University of Warwick found

that happiness led to a 12% spike in productivity, while unhappy workers proved 10% less productive. As the research team put it, "We find that human happiness has large and positive causal effects on productivity. Positive emotions appear to invigorate human beings." (Fastcompany.com, Jonha Revesencio 07/22/15)

Awareness is the first step to change. Most of us recognize when something is not working. The most common response to that, however, is that we keep our heads down and continue to put one foot in front of the other, just like we always have. We may complain that things aren't right; we may gossip about who we think is at fault and form cliques with others who agree with us because misery loves company. But this creates division, and division breaks apart families, communities, and countries, as well as businesses. Diversity and division are two entirely different things. Diversity adds variety, different perspectives, and the magnificence of learning to look at things in a new light. Division just creates walls that "need" to be protected, causing dissention, alienation, and dissolution.

It's not a bad thing to recognize that things aren't working. Again, awareness of the problem is important; but complaining and doing the same things over and over while expecting different results is a sign of insanity, according to Albert Einstein. Yet that's exactly what we do.

We believe that we can keep our home and work lives separate. Our employers actually expect us to do that, too. And when we get home, our spouses, partners, kids, and friends expect us to leave work at the office. It seems to me that it's easier said than done.

Because I think this is difficult to do, I asked the experts. I spoke to business people whom I admire and asked them to be honest and frank about their thoughts regarding what contributes to workplace stress and dissatisfaction. I asked if they thought personal problems contribute to problems in the workplace, and I heard a resounding "Yes!" When people are experiencing stressors in their personal lives, it's very difficult to stay focused on the task at hand. And when they aren't focused, things fall through the cracks, deadlines are missed, and sick leave gets out of hand.

One of the business owners that I spoke to acknowledges that "these issues are always at hand, and good management recognizes that." You can't pretend it doesn't exist and not do anything to resolve this problem, but still expect quality results.

If Zentivity is a peaceful, calm environment in which employees are actively engaged in the creative and productive process so that they can make more money and everyone can be happy and well-motivated, we need to take a look at what inhibits that.

What leads to *less* Zentivity? Feelings of captivity, negativity, projectivity and reactivity.

Captivity

Feeling trapped can make anyone unhappy or anxious, either in one's personal life or at work. Whether it is in a relationship or a dead-end job, this feeling of constriction and limited options can lead to frustration, anger, lashing out, or just escaping. The latter is often attempted in a variety of ways, such as self-medicating with alcohol, drugs, or food, or through extramarital affairs or disconnecting emotionally, which leads to all kinds of unhealthy communication patterns and behaviors. When people feel that they are in captivity, they can lose their motivation to be engaged or take care of themselves physically. In the extreme case, imagine how it would feel to be in a concentration camp where someone else is in control of when and what you eat, when and how you work, when and if you sleep, and who you talk to. And that someone doesn't care how you feel about any of that.

Negativity

It's easy to slip into despair and become addicted to negativity when you feel powerless, believe you are not being heard or validated, or struggle to make ends meet. You can easily fall prey to it yourself, or you can be caught up in an environment in which others are held in its hypnotic trance. It manifests in many ways, such as constant complaining, gossiping, whining, feeling weighed down, experiencing insecurity, or focusing on what's not working instead of looking for solutions. In your job, if you are focused on what is not working or what hasn't worked in the past but neglect to look for solutions, then you find yourself and your department living in the past and not moving forward, which of course will lead to decreased productivity.

Projectivity

When people are unable to take responsibility for their own feelings and actions, they often project their own negativity or bad feelings on others. They will accuse those around them of the feelings that they actually disown in themselves.

"Why are you always so angry?" you ask your boss.

"You're the one who's angry."

"Who me?" you bellow. "I am *not angry*! Dammit!"

We all know someone who does this. Always complaining about how rude or inconsiderate everyone is to them, they fail to recognize the behavior or attitude that they themselves show to others. This can easily be seen in drivers experiencing road rage or people who never get their reports in on time.

Projectivity is a way of refusing to take personal responsibility by blaming others for unacknowledged feelings in oneself.

Reactivity

Those knee-jerk reactions that just come out before you think things through…do you know anyone in your office who does that? Do you have certain automatic reactions? Anger, revulsion, judgment, annoyance? How do we keep from expressing them?

Holocaust survivor Viktor Frankl says, "Between stimulus and response there is a space. In that space is our power to choose our response. In our response lies our growth and our freedom." You will learn how to identify that space in which reactive emotions and behaviors are triggered, and how to put a cushion of detachment in between the stimulus and the reaction, so that you have control over your response and experience better results.

The purpose of this book is to help you recognize troubling emotions, patterns, and reactions before they grow out of control and not only damage your personal relationships, but your professional reputation and effectiveness.

Everything you do is
changing the world.
Every word. Every
thought.
Every action.
What does your impact
look like?

Marianne Clyde

- marianneclyde.com

CHAPTER 2

You Can't Run When Your Feet Are Stuck

Through talking to business owners, I discovered that the list of personal problems keeping employees mired in fear—feelings of captivity and negativity—seems endless.

Divorce or marital problems, financial strain, and employee or family member health issues are all on that list. But then again, so are pregnancy and upcoming weddings.

As you can see, not all family issues are negative; some are happy and fun. Yet good or bad, they increase stress levels, providing an opportunity for lack of focus, distraction, or extensive time spent on the phone or computer. All potential energy that ideally would be on the task at hand is diverted and watered down when employees don't practice healthy coping mechanisms, good communication, and conflict resolution skills. And of course, the company needs to provide good communication structure and clear guidelines to keep things as predictable as possible and offer ways to handle the unpredictable.

One of the business owners said, "Secrets are the death of morale because for staff, they mean that management does not trust them." This business owner has 60–90 employees, depending on the season. It is a high-service industry, so if employees are unhappy, chances are huge that negativity will trickle down to the customers, which in turn trickles down to the community, establishing a negative reputation for the business and impacting sales.

Another business owner stresses the need for both happy employees and customers because the "YELP culture" is very stressful. Disgruntled customers and employees can use this online platform to air their grievances, which can damage a company's reputation and ultimately its profits.

Living in Fear

So fear hovers over employees who may not trust management because "secrets" might mean that they are being talked about and not included in the company's future plans. It makes them feel on edge and insecure.

And business owners have to constantly monitor their reputation online where one bad review by a disgruntled employee or customer can take years to redeem. According to the software company Zendesk, this is a valid concern since 88% of customers indicate that they have been influenced by an online customer service review when making a buying decision. While you may not be able to control everything posted online, you can certainly lay the groundwork to minimize negative reviews and unhappy employees, which can influence how a customer feels about your business.

Fear is also present when an employee has to struggle to make ends meet. The focus is not on this particular job, but on looking for another higher-paying job or working a second job. One observant business owner noticed that a particular employee was often quick-tempered and close to tears due to financial pressures. While this employee was doing her best not to let that spill over into her customer service, a wise business owner pays attention and asks questions. Straightforward, direct, and kind communication can solve many problems before they get out of hand.

There is no doubt that sooner or later, the employee's stress levels will cause distraction. For example, she might seek a second job. While this might meet the immediate need of allaying fears about finances, this employee was already working at full capacity, so where would she find time to juggle a second job? The employer wasn't sure. But because the employer addressed the situation before stress levels got out of hand, she provided a safe environment for the employee to discuss her problems, and together they found a way to restructure her pay so that it was more predictable, relieving fears of a less-than-steady income. The stress was immediately lifted from the employee, and the open, trusting communication with the employer set a precedent of flexibility and feelings of a safer, more secure environment.

However, keep in mind that it is not your job to "fix" every employee problem, financial or otherwise. It's important to recognize that your employees should have the ability to figure out their own problems. As the employer, you can offer a safe space to explore those options and offer suggestions, but the employee should choose which option works best for her.

As in any healthy relationship, it's important to hold steady when the other person experiences strong emotions. They might need to struggle with fear, anger, or any other emotion before they work out what is best. You can't fix it by taking away the fear; neither can you fix it by taking on the fear yourself. Hold steady; be kind and flexible if possible, but detach enough to let the other person work out his or her own solution.

Feeling Trapped

When employees feel trapped by finances or lack of opportunity, work begins to look like a prison that inhibits their growth and freedom. Most employees bristle under this feeling of captivity.

Some business leaders address the issue of employees feeling "handcuffed" by a variety of things. Sometimes it is the closing time at day care, where they charge you extra or even kick your child out if you are late too many times. The tension between the need to finish a job and the need to pick up a child creates a lot of stress.

In addition, an employee or executive can feel handcuffed by a contract that is no longer being honored or involves changed circumstances. So it is important to address these changes in circumstances and make modifications when necessary.

On the other hand, one employer indicates that some of his 16 employees actually want "handcuffs" so they don't have to take ownership and be responsible for their actions. However, employees who do take ownership and feel some responsibility for the outcome are far more invested in the company's success and enjoy their work more.

Negativity is Contagious

These feelings of fear or captivity can cause discomfort that spreads: employees begin to mumble under their breath, whisper to other employees, or form cliques that make it difficult to get work done in a synergistic manner. Underlying discontent and lack of communication with managers are important causes of negativity.

But there are also those who bring negativity to the workplace with personal issues of anger, reactivity, and defensiveness that can wreak havoc with relationships among employees. Simply put, if an employee has a personality issue that is causing trouble at home—gossip, anger, sense of superiority, or entitlement—chances are good that it will cause problems at work, and vice versa. Learning good communication skills is vital because habits that create knee-jerk reactions perpetuate themselves. Reactivity and anger lead to defensiveness and projectivity; the combination creates a spiral that turns into a tornado of unhealthy feelings and reactions, while the focus on the job at hand gets lost in the fray.

PART TWO
Creating the Solution

You recognize that
tightness in your chest?
That nausea in your
stomach?
The way you are gritting
your teeth?

Those are signs that you
are blocking your flow of
energy.
It has nothing to do with
the person that offended
you, hurt you,
disregarded you.
It has only to do with
you.

Picture the tightness in
your body, then send an
arrow of light and watch
it disperse.
Let it go.
Not because what they
did was OK, but because
you are.

Marianne Clyde

- marianneclyde.com

CHAPTER 3

Becoming Proactive

This section is about how we actually create change in our lives. And let's just get this out up front: you don't make change by continually talking about how bad the problem is. As a matter of fact, that simply makes things worse. If we continue to focus on the problem, it will increase and never go away. We often link so strongly with the problem that it becomes part of our identity.

I am depressed. I'm broke. I hate the lady in the next cubicle. Do you ever find yourself in that trap? Yes, we absolutely have to identify the problem, but only so we know what we have to fix. We don't focus on it to bring blame or to shame anyone. We name it so we can know what to aim for and bring resolution.

Once we have identified the problem, we can set ourselves on the path to resolve it. We need to identify where we want to go.

If we don't want reactivity, negativity, projectivity, or captivity, what is it that we *do* want? How about connectivity, sensitivity, objectivity, activity, creativity, and productivity?

Connectivity

When there is a thriving synergy in our workplaces, things get done quickly and efficiently, and are often wrapped in an added layer of fun. We like to feel good and included. We like to sense that our contribution is not only accepted, but sought out and valued.

Free to ask questions and consider thoughts that hadn't crossed our minds before, we embrace a new way of thinking and keep our systems flexible and running through economy changes, governmental upsets, and the ever-winding thread of shifting regulations and expectations. The rigid reed breaks.

Connecting with our team in a way where everyone is heard and respected, we find that we become more adaptable to change. When joining with others in a constructive way, making the most of our diversity, personality differences, and variety of skills and talents, we create a better product or service.

One of my favorite movies is *Divergent*, a story of the rebuilding of a society that has nearly been destroyed by an apocalyptic war. Convinced that people must be divided into homogeneous groups in order for them to be safe and controllable, the powers that be create societal sectors, each with their own specific job. If they show strength or interest in more than one sector, they are sought out and destroyed.

But as it turns out, the ones who are "divergent" (gifted in more than one area) are more capable of integrating a variety of thought processes and freer ways of thinking. The reason they are destroyed is that they pose a threat to the control of the powers that be. Fear of change and loss of control are actually what create the chaos, not diverse ways of thinking. When we connect a diverse group of employees who are all accountable in some way for the outcome, the result is better productivity.

In her 2016 Gallup article, Amy Adkins states, "Gallup categorizes workers as engaged based on their ratings of key workplace elements—such as having an opportunity to do what they do best each day, having someone at work who encourages their development and believing their opinions count at work—that predict important organizational performance outcomes. Engaged employees are involved in, enthusiastic about, and committed to their work. Gallup's extensive research shows that employee engagement is strongly connected to business outcomes essential to an organization's financial success, such as productivity, profitability, and customer engagement. Engaged employees drive the innovation, growth, and revenue that their companies need."

Sensitivity

We certainly don't want to create an office full of crybabies! Sometimes it seems like we have gotten to the point where we are bothered by everything, and we don't have the sense or the skills to resolve issues. So we need to become aware by noticing and respecting our own thoughts and feelings as well as those of others; realizing what's going on around us; practicing mindfulness and gratitude; and noticing the needs of others. One business owner said that "[the employees] will almost always give you more than you gave them, just by understanding their issues." He reminds us of the Stephen Covey quote, "Seek first to understand and then to be understood."

Objectivity

Simply focusing on breathing helps one to detach from the emotion of the moment. Resisting the need to be defensive opens up an opportunity to create a dialog so that you can hear what the other person is saying and in turn, be heard. When this happens, you create an atmosphere of respect and cooperation, recognizing and respecting personality differences as well as differing strengths and weaknesses. There's room for everyone's ideas, whether you agree with them or not. If you are curious instead of judgmental, you find that there is always something new to learn.

The brain changes when we learn to see things differently. And learning to see things from different perspectives makes you more empathetic and flexible. You find that there actually exists more that the two options that seem very familiar to you: my way or the highway. You might find that the scenic route is often much more effective, even though it may take longer. Remove yourself from the emotion and drama of the moment by breathing. Strong emotions such as fear, anger, and defensiveness inhibit the brain from functioning at full capacity. When you get sucked into the drama, emotion takes over reason, and it's less likely that a productive decision will be made.

Activity

Activity is not the same as busy-ness. I am talking about focused, well-thought-out activity, which comes from a place of calm. Using cooperation and a sense of community, where credit is given to the team rather than just to the bosses, executives, and managers, inspires employees to become invested in the process. They feel respected and important. And when employees feel like they are making a difference, with their ideas being heard and validated, it keeps them involved, active, and mentally stimulated.

Mental stimulation is vital to mental health and growth, creating an overall sense of well-being. In addition, it's important to note that physical fitness and healthy eating affects the brain, which affects the body, which affects productivity. I have noticed companies that encourage taking care of one's physical health have employees that are more energetic, take care of themselves, and feel better about themselves.

Creativity

Believe it or not, you have everything within you to create anything you want. Creativity involves learning to be open to brainstorming and new ways of thinking that keep a business alive and vibrant. A healthy business does everything it can to encourage creativity and open people up enough to share their ideas, knowing that they will be heard and validated. This doesn't mean a business leader has to use every idea that comes his or her way, but it does mean listening without judgment and being curious about new ideas.

Productivity

You want your company to make more widgets, earn more money, and generate your products and services with efficiency and abundance, so what's stopping you?

What are the things that seem to interfere with productivity at your office? What seems to put a glitch in the smooth flow of efficiency at home? You might think that it's your boss or your coworkers. You might blame your crowded schedule filled with everyone else's needs and not yours. Perhaps you're tempted to blame God, the devil, or your health.

However, rather than looking for something or someone to blame, let's take another approach. Sometimes even the suggestion to look at things differently causes people to feel resentful because it feels like you are not being validated for how crazy your environment feels to you and how stuck you feel—not to mention how angry and annoyed you are.

I hear you. And I do understand how overwhelming life seems; however, it's my job *not* to let you stay there with your head spinning and your anger boiling. Of course you can, and some people do decide to stay overwhelmed, or locked in anger, resentment, fear, anxiety, or depression because they feel like they are justified in feeling that way.

And you *may* be justified in feeling that way, but the point is and should remain that you want to feel more productive. You want to learn how to communicate better so that you get heard and feel validated and not overwhelmed.

That cannot and will not happen if you continue to focus on

your negative feelings, or your reasons for not getting there, no matter how valid those reasons or excuses are.

When you take responsibility for your feelings and understand that it is *your beliefs* about those circumstances that are causing you the most stress, then you are in a powerful position that enables you to change.

So when you are focused on the negative aspects of your job, such as the irritations and inconveniences, you have less energy to apply to the job at hand. Your brain is a million miles away from what makes you feel worthy or accomplished or good at your job, which leads to less productivity.

When you can be more sensitive and aware of others' feelings or how your work is being affected by outside circumstances, you can better focus on where you want to go and what you want to accomplish.

Taking the time to connect with other employees with respect and cooperation, you will find that there are fewer obstacles to face and more synergy in your workplace. You will find that you can be more objective by backing up and taking that deep breath, allowing you to detach from the drama, which is an energy-sucker.

When you release things that cause stress and distraction, you allow more room in your day for creativity and productive activity, leading you in the direction that you ultimately want to go.

The 10 Essential Principles

Connect to Your Creator
Know Your True Identity
Nurture Awareness
Breathe
Respect
Practice Gratitude
Limit Judgments
Detach
Communicate Clearly
Forgive Quickly

- marianneclyde.com

CHAPTER 4

Principles to Keep You Centered and Focused

Ten principles that can be applied at home and at work, and are foundational for living a life of Zentivity are:

Connect to Your Creator
Know Your True Identity
Nurture Awareness
Breathe
Respect
Practice Gratitude
Limit Judgments
Detach
Communicate Clearly
Forgive Quickly

When you live these principles, you enhance your awareness, which of course is the beginning of change, and lays a firm foundation of rock-solid calm from which you can propel yourself to a life of healthy relationships and a workplace that is pleasant and productive.

Sure, it can be easy to get sidetracked and slip off course, or to let a small problem evolve into a big mess, or a big problem turn into chaos. But you can always turn back to these 10 universal principles, which are beneficial in every area of life in reducing stress, chaos, and discontent. They help you establish that internal locus of control, which is so important in developing healthy relationships, making good decisions, and creating thoughtful, wise responses to stressful situations that arise at home or in the workplace. These principles can serve as your guide to giving you more control in creating the life and environment that you desire.

Connect to Your Creator

The first principle is connection; the most important one you can make is with the creator, your source, the universe, or God. It means plugging into all that is wisdom and truth, love and joy, peace and abundance. This is your normal state of being, despite what you may believe. You might think that your normal state is one of anxiety, anger, tension, irritation, or busy-ness, but that is not true. Your normal state—the one in which you are most comfortable and productive—is one where you feel calm, joyful, abundant, and absolutely fearless. Because in this state, there is nothing to be afraid of. Nothing can hurt you or throw you off balance. Can you see the importance of plugging into this state of being at least a couple of times each day? This is done by simply disconnecting from everything else and focusing on your connection to all that is. Take some time to stop whatever you're doing and listen to the quiet. Consciously tap into the wisdom within you. Slowly breathe in love, joy, peace, and wisdom, and breathe out stress, anger, confusion, and fear. If you can do that for 20 minutes twice a day, great. If you can only do it while you're in the shower, then go with that. Perhaps you can find a minute or two at a stoplight. Just begin to be conscious of the fact that you are one with the energy that creates life.

Once you connect with this energy, you can connect with yourself and know your true identity. Until you do so, it's difficult to connect with others. The reason is simple. If you are hiding bits of yourself from yourself, which we all have done, you can't share yourself with others. You are self-protective, defensive, or inauthentic in some way. If this is the case, you cannot fully be present for someone else. But once you connect with yourself, it becomes easier to connect with and unconditionally love others, and be in a relationship that is non-reactive and completely proactive and open. It's so much easier to connect with someone who is authentic and absolutely at ease with himself. There is no defensiveness, posturing, or manipulation necessary.

Spending time marinating in the connection to the divine, the source of all things, creates a groundedness that is inaccessible except by your awareness of it. It's already there, but if you don't plug into it, the power and peace is unavailable to you. It's really no different than a lamp that is unplugged. It may be a beautiful lamp with a brand new bulb, but if it's not plugged in, it's not going to work. You hold the plug, and only you can connect it to an outlet.

When you take a few minutes a day to do that, it sheds new light on your relationships, which in turn reflect in the rest of your life, including your success and productivity at work.

Know Your True Identity

In my counseling and coaching practice, I always start out with the assumption that you are whole, perfect, and complete—all the way down to your core. Now you might not believe me or you might think, "Yeah, but I don't *feel* whole, perfect, or complete."

When you know your *true identity*, you don't have to pretend to be anything or anyone else. When you know your purpose for living, you aren't distressed by what others think. When you are aware that you are connected to something bigger than the petty, moody, and often changing opinions of others, it's not very easy to get thrown off course. And even if you do get temporarily thrown off, you know exactly what to do to get back on track.

It's not that you don't get hurt or angry or frustrated anymore, but you don't live there. You don't give anyone else the right to live in your head and control your thoughts by making you feel a certain way. You take ownership of your feelings and know that you alone are responsible for them, not someone or something outside of yourself. If you are the one responsible for your anger or feeling offended, all you have to do in order to feel differently is to change the thoughts that prompt that feeling.

When you understand that you are one with the energy that is love, joy, peace, patience, goodness, self-control, wisdom, creativity, and abundance, it's easier to see that you *are* those things. That is your true nature. Your awareness is the plug. Once you are plugged in, it sheds light on the truth, which is that you are amazing and indestructible.

Nurture Awareness

When we nurture our awareness, we get to know ourselves and our surroundings in an intimate way. We learn what makes us tick, how we feel about things, and what triggers an emotional reaction. We become aware of our impact on the environment and on other people.

Awareness is the beginning of change. You can't change something that you don't know exists or that you are denying. So becoming aware allows us to honestly and objectively examine who we are and who we want to be. Feeling secure, we are able to see ourselves with a critical eye, creating behaviors and responses that are healthy and loving, where they might not have been so in the past.

I'm not referring to just personal insight; awareness is becoming aware of what is going on around us. We can observe it and embrace it for what it is and make wise decisions accordingly. We can learn to enjoy our surroundings and engage with people in a way that is kind and loving without judgment. Having no need to fix or label anyone else, we can just enjoy what is.

It's important to note that these concepts are not magic, as pointed out by a couple of business owners. One runs a busy hardware company and another owns a successful construction company. Like most of us, they talk about having good weeks and bad weeks. During good weeks, personal relationships fly high and their businesses seem easy and relatively stress-free.

Don, the owner of the construction company, says, "When I'm calm, our jobsites are fun! We enjoy being around each other. All of my guys have been around for an average of 15 years, and clearly, when I have a good handle on things, production is absolutely more efficient. I track productivity by the number of units produced. How many bricks did we lay? If my guys lay more bricks, we get finished quicker and move on to the next job. That piles up in a hurry!"

"This kind of productivity happens when I meditate," he continues. "When I don't, I get impatient and snap at them. They get reactive and resentful and shut down." So there is a clear correlation of the importance of Don's quiet time each day and his company's bottom line. The correlation of staying *aware* of how he's feeling, taking personal responsibility, and how he treats his employees is key.

The same goes for Steve, the hardware store owner. "When I meditate, things just go better," he says. "When I don't, I get depressed and anxious, and am not as easy to work for."

Breathe

My mantra, as anyone who knows me will tell you, is to "just breathe…" It's tattooed on my wrist.

Breathing is our constant reminder that we are connected to life in an intimate way. Taking a deep breath when we are stressed is an invitation to calm down and step back. Conscious breathing gets the oxygen flowing through our bodies, bringing life and health to all our organs. Deep breathing allows us to exhale toxins. It reduces anxiety and depression, helps us sleep, reduces pain, enables us to regulate our emotions, and helps limit impulsivity and reactiveness.

Jane, who works for a busy government contracting business, says that despite high stress levels at work, she is now better able to cope by stepping back and taking a deep breath. She says, "I don't find myself spun up emotionally all the time, ruminating about conflicts and disappointments, so these principles have enabled me to be more efficient with time, which of course, contributes to productivity. These techniques have allowed me to listen to the voice in my head that calms me down. I am more able to separate from the drama, stepping back and seeing things from others' perspectives, which helps me modify my behavior accordingly."

Respect

Respect is so important on many levels: respect for self, for others, for nature, and for differences in opinion and viewpoints. As with every other principle, it begins with learning to respect ourselves so that we can truly respect others. If we don't respect ourselves, our response to other people is skewed, and they treat us like we expect to be treated. And if we don't respect ourselves, we have no governor on our expectations about how others can, should, or will treat us.

If we are completely comfortable with and respectful of ourselves, we have no triggers that others can tap into. We have no reason to feel superior or inferior. We respect ourselves and others equally. As a matter of fact, we respect all things: all of nature and creation, recognizing that we are one with the creator and with all things.

Life is so much more relaxing when we are in a good place personally. There's no need to judge or mistreat others. We can allow things to unfold naturally and understand that everyone is in his or her own place in this journey we call life. In eternity, there is no beginning or end, so with our eternal selves, you really can't tell who is ahead of you or behind you. It's best to just allow things to unfold, moving in the direction you feel led to go, allowing others to do the same.

Practice Gratitude

When we understand that we are one with all things, it's easy to be grateful for all things. When we comprehend that we are one with the creator, it becomes easier to enjoy the life that we are living, knowing that it has purpose and order, even if it doesn't feel that way at the moment.

A regular practice of gratitude changes your brain for the better. Thinking of three things to be grateful for before you get out of bed in the morning and three things as you lay your head on your pillow at night puts parentheses of thankfulness around your whole life and becomes a lifestyle of thanksgiving, setting the stage for abundance. When you are grateful for what you have, you attract more. If you are always complaining about what you don't have or what you need or want, you attract more scarcity into your life. This follows the principles that what you resist persists, and what you focus on increases.

Limit Judgments

We've all been around judgmental people. You know them—they always have an opinion about everyone and everything, and it's rarely positive. Judgment breeds discontent and negativity. Since these are things we seek to eliminate in the workplace, in our homes, and in our lives in general, it's better to focus on what we do want. Yes, we need discernment, but that is different from judgment. Discernment is observing and making a wise decision based on the information at hand. It doesn't have to be a decision between good and bad, but rather what would benefit the current direction you want to follow.

We live in a world of win/lose. What would it look like if we could live in a world of win/win? If something is good, we automatically assume something else is bad. What if it was all good? Or better yet, what if it just is what it is—with no judgment attached at all? It may seem like a fantasy, but remember, good or bad is in the eye of the perceiver. How you perceive what you consider your reality determines how you respond to it.

In our workplaces, this negative approach to life and situations creates conflict and discontent. What if we were able to at least ask the new question, "What if?" What if that idea worked? What if we could implement that new thought? What if we tried? What if?

Detach

Wouldn't it be great to be able to step back and see things differently for a change? So often we find ourselves caught up in drama and emotion. Both at home and at work, we have a tendency to get sucked in, and it's easy to understand why. It's because you are the same person in both places. While at work, you might be able to hold back emotional and reactive responses because the stakes are high and you don't want to lose your job. But the stakes are high at home, too.

In both settings, learning to step outside of yourself to become an observer instead of a player limits reactiveness, automatic judgments, and habitual emotional responses. This creates a small cushion of space between you and the situation at hand, which gives you an extra second or so to help you determine a wise and healthy response. This goes a long way toward preventing things from spiraling out of control.

This moment of detachment or disengagement keeps you from reacting with an unconscious behavior. It could be used in a situation where you are tempted to reach for one too many drinks, an extra bag of chips, a second or third donut. It can also be used to prevent a defensive reaction such as a biting comment, letting fly a nasty word or accusation, or reaching out to punch a wall, slam a cupboard, or even strike a child. It stops those unconscious actions that you can't take back once they leave your lips or you lash out physically. It gives a moment for you to regain control of your response, which can save you ripples of regret.

When you are immersed in a negative or reactive mode, your IQ drops—it's true! Your brain is not processing in a mature manner, and you risk saying or doing something you regret. When you detach from the drama and intensity of the moment, what comes out of your mouth will be calmer, and the chances of a more positive outcome increase.

Communicate Clearly

I have one basic communication premise that once accomplished, you will find that in addition to your communication seeming easier and more authentic, you also won't worry as much about what people think or if you said the "right" thing or not.

That premise is to get grounded. It is based on the connection that you make with all that is so you can know your true identity. Fall in love with, respect, and enjoy your true self. Once you do this, connecting with others is easy.

But until you do this, communicating with other people will always be difficult. You will continue to worry about how people are interpreting what you say and wonder if they sense your true intention. You will experience feelings of rejection if they disagree with you, or correct or judge you.

Unless you connect with and learn to live from your truest self, which will enable you to develop a stronger internal locus of control, where you are in charge, you will never really feel grounded. Your feelings will continue to be determined by external things, which feels a little bit like being tossed around in a tornado. When you learn who you really are and begin to move in real authenticity, you will feel grounded and secure at all times.

Learning to communicate effectively is a powerful relational tool that can enhance well-being and performance in the workplace. Examples of strong communication skills include reflective listening skills, eye-contact, taking ownership of one's feelings, and speaking to be understood.

When I talk about reactive behavior patterns with clients, they often say, "That's just the way I am." What that says to me is that they have no interest in changing, or at least they don't see the importance of backing off from a situation and becoming an observer. They don't understand how impactful it can be to detach from drama, if even for a moment, and redirect the conversation in a healthier and more productive direction. It's well worth it to have occasional team building and skill-enhancing workshops for employees to help them strengthen these techniques.

Forgive Quickly

Maybe you've heard it said that un-forgiveness is like drinking poison and expecting the other person to die. Well, it's true.

One of the most difficult things to do as a therapist is to help someone who is convinced that they have the right to hold a grudge, to let it go and forgive. In my view, forgiveness benefits the offended as much or more than the offender.

To understand what forgiveness really is, it's important to understand what it is not. It isn't a license for the person to hurt or offend you again, nor is it a release from guilt. It doesn't say that what the offender did was okay or that it was inconsequential. It doesn't mean that some things might not have to change or that restitution might not be required. It doesn't even mean that you have to remain in relationship with the offender.

What it does is release you from carrying that burden of hate, anger, or pain. When stressful emotions take over, hormones including cortisol and adrenalin are released. If they run their course and are released in optimal amounts, they can help you get through a stressful time or get away from a dangerous situation. However, when we are in a constant or frequent state of stress, these hormones are released continually, and our bodies must find something to do with them. What happens? They can affect our blood sugar levels, inhibit our immune systems, and cause stomach or heart issues as well as other health problems. That's why "walking it off" is an important way to deal with stress. It gives our body a chance to release these hormones in a healthy way.

When we hold onto a stress-inducing emotion like hatred, anger, disgust, resentment, depression, or anxiety, which is often how un-forgiveness manifests, we create health problems for ourselves. When our muscles are in a constant state of tension, the hormones causing it become toxic. So un-forgiveness truly is poison for your body.

Forgiveness is a choice. You don't have to wait until you feel joyful about the other person, but choosing to release their offense to a higher power is a good place to start so that you can be free. As long as you are tied to resentment, you cannot be free inside, and that may lead you to holding back in your relationships and potentially in your work.

Learning to practice and implement these 10 Essential Principles in your life, you can stand strong, even if people don't respond as you hope and circumstances seems less than optimal.

If Jim and Anna had only used these principles…

In their social circles, Jim and Anna are admired as the perfect couple. They have three wonderful kids who are good students, involved in community sports, take music lessons, and have plenty of friends. Anna and Jim both have good jobs and make good incomes. They are on a variety of nonprofit boards and involved in good causes in the community.

They fell in love as college students. Anna came from a middle-income family that was very active and well-known in their community. Dad was a businessman; mom was a teacher. They took family vacations every summer and had dinner together every night. There was never any fighting in their house. It was generally quiet, with everybody doing his or her own thing. She doesn't remember her parents ever fighting.

Sometimes her brother was a little bossy and abusive when they were kids and she felt a little left out as the middle child, but for the most part, it was a calm, predictable childhood.

Jim, on the other hand, was raised by a fiercely loving and emotional single mother. She worked two jobs to provide for her cherished son. Because of the many work hours, she was often exhausted and sometimes reactive. She had migraines and often napped in a dark room until they passed. Jim occupied himself by reading, watching TV, or playing with his friends. In high school, he was a football hero and adored by all the girls. Mom couldn't make it to many games, but she saved all his news clippings and bragged about him to her friends. Sometimes he and his mom got into some pretty loud fights, but by the next day, all was forgotten.

When they met, Jim fell in love with Anna's calm demeanor and appreciated how well the family seemed to function. Anna was attracted to his feisty personality and loved how self-sufficient he was. It seemed to be a match made in heaven. And it was.

Eventually they got married and things were great. Jim was a self-made businessman and worked hard. Often he worked long hours and had difficulty finding time to take a day off, let alone a couple of weeks at a time.

Anna had a teaching job that she liked. It was predictable, and she had summers off, a great opportunity for fun vacations. But Jim could never go. She didn't say anything because she knew he was working hard and she admired that. But Anna often found herself alone. "This isn't how families operate," she thought to herself. "Families go on vacation. Families eat dinner together every night. If he loved me, he would find time for me."

As the years passed, these feelings intensified. With the arrival of children, it became clear to Anna that Jim didn't even care about them. He was rarely home for dinner, and she ended up having to keep the plates spinning by herself. But she kept her thoughts to herself, becoming more and more withdrawn.

When Jim actually did come home, he found Anna and the kids already in bed, or she'd be on the phone with a friend. Sometimes she would be engrossed in a TV show and shush him if he tried to talk or give her a hug. Jim started to feel rejected and unloved. "I work hard every day to show her how much I love her, but she doesn't care." He tried to talk and she responded angrily, "Why do you always have to make everything in to a fight?" "What fight? I'm just trying to talk. We never talk about stuff," he snorted and stomped out of the room. "If she loved me," he thought to himself, "she would engage in some way."

Over the years, they grew farther apart. She took care of the kids, sometimes even taking them on vacations without him. She never said much, but underneath, she was seething and judging him for being a neglectful husband and bad father. These thoughts led to much stress in her life. She is the one who always had to take off work to take the kids to the doctor or to their games. She stopped asking him to help because she believed that he didn't care. "Fine. I'll just do it myself."

Anna found herself stressed out at work. Because she was a special education teacher, her job seemed more stressful than that of the other teachers, so she started feeling sorry for herself. She didn't ask for help at work either. Her belief was that you shouldn't have to ask; people should innately understand and pitch in. So she became more resentful at work and less responsive at home.

Feeling unwelcome at home, Jim worked even more and then met friends at the bar for a drink. They appreciated a good debate and never seemed to get offended. His belief was that if people debate and connect with you on an emotional level, you are valuable. If not, they just don't care. Who wants to be around a woman who doesn't care?

Anna found that she was sick much of the time and ended up taking too much time off from work. She got passed up for a promotion that she had been "promised" a couple of years ago "whenever the job opened up." So she got mad and quit.

When the economy took a nosedive, it affected Jim's ability to bring in as much money as in prior years. The financial pressure led him to lay off workers, which made it difficult to get the work done. Because

Anna had quit her job in a rage, she cut off her ability to find a new one in that school district.

Both Jim and Anna fell prey to a couple of common situations. One is that they came from different home "cultures," assuming that each was the way it was "supposed" to be. They each had different ways of feeling loved. Hers was in the predictability of family life, even though nobody talked about things much. You just "sucked it up" and moved on…until you just couldn't anymore. Jim felt loved when emotions were high and you spent all your time working. They became like two ships passing in the night, each feeling inadequate and unloved because they weren't having their expectations met. So they put their noses to the grindstone and kept doing the same things over and over, hoping things would change. Because they really didn't understand the dynamics behind their feelings, they had difficulty talking about it, and they opted to shut down and build a wall protecting themselves.

Because both thought they were right, they blamed their problems on the other, creating a defensive posturing situation, where someone has to win and someone has to lose. As the stress increased without being addressed, it affected Anna's health and her job. Circumstances in the economy affected Jim's job, which caused him to feel inadequate. His solution was to work harder until he burnt himself out. Neither one felt validated or supported by the other. Their expectations were based on things outside of themselves: the economy, his wife, her husband, her job, their belief system about the way things "should be done."

Yet their belief systems came from their childhoods—neither one was wrong. One wasn't better than the other. They were just unexamined. They moved in unawareness that they were running on subconscious assumptions, without realizing that they could change that.

But our beliefs can't change until we become aware of them. Our knee-jerk reactions don't change until we choose to change them.

And if we don't become aware of these things, we continue to defend them because although not comfortable, at least they are familiar.

Posturing and defensiveness come from a sense of insecurity. And it does not stop until you take time to be still and learn to appreciate how amazing you are, without all your cultural beliefs and habits and thought processes. Your family is not what makes you special, nor is your position in the family. Your job, or how hard you work, or your beliefs don't make you special either.

What makes you special is just the fact that you exist. And the one who truly knows that better than anyone is the one who created you. That's why that connection is primary. It's an important foundation.

Because Jim and Anna's sense of well-being and security was based on something other than that, something changeable and unsteady, when the pressure was on, they found that their footing faltered.

If Jim and Anna had talked things through and forgiven each other, they would have been in a better position to move beyond their current circumstances, rather than being sucked down into a spiral of despair that created unproductive outcomes not only in their family, but in their places of employment as well.

If you find yourself
stuck,
perhaps you stepped on a
piece of un-forgiveness.
All you need to do is
scrape it off and
get on your way.

Marianne Clyde

- marianneclyde.com

CHAPTER 5

Communicating to Connect

It becomes simple when *you* are your control center rather than everything and everyone else. When you are constantly reacting to the whims of others, the winds of circumstances, and the tides of change, you feel tossed around like a scrap of paper in a windstorm. In that case, you are subject to an external locus of control, which means you are a victim of the needs, desires, and opinions of others. You are at the mercy of other people's moods, panic, stress, and deadlines. You often find yourself subject to angry judgmental people or even an angry, demanding, exacting God with a laundry list of how you keep messing up. So you stay a little off balance, always trying to dance to a tune that something or someone outside of you is playing, changing randomly at any moment—like a never-ending game of musical chairs.

Can you see how this could interfere with your communication patterns and your relationships? If you always try to stay one step ahead of the one you are communicating with, trying to read his or her mind or figure out what he or she wants you to say so that will lead to the raise, the response, or the affirmation you want or need, you will always be anxious. You will send out vibes that you're not really focused on the relationship. In other words, you are not really communicating purposefully, you are simply reacting to stimuli.

It's important to validate the one you are communicating with because if you shut him down with invalidation and push your own agenda without caring what's important to him, he'll never hear what you have to say. He will shut down. He might talk and even answer your questions, but communicate? No!

You win or lose someone's attention within the first couple of seconds of engagement. If you are interested and address what's important to him, you become magnetic to him.

Make sure you listen. It's the most important skill in communication. Don't cut in with advice or opinion. Don't play "Can You Top This?" Don't let your eyes or attention wander. Just listen with the intent to understand. Keep the following tips in mind:

1. Give whomever you are communicating with your full attention. Your body posture is facing them and open.
2. Maintain gentle eye contact. Do not allow your eyes to wander or look for someone or something else more interesting. This can be difficult and takes practice, but if you are trying to make someone else feel valued, face-to-face communication with kind eye contact is essential. This is true with employees, coworkers, superiors, or your family. As a general rule, people know you are present with them emotionally if you have good eye contact. There are cultural exceptions of course, but generally in Western culture, eye contact is considered to be a way to gauge trustworthiness.
3. Put all electronic devices out of sight.

Now that you are positioned to listen, here are some important points on *how* to listen:

1. Give regular indications that you are paying attention. Nod, say "Mhmm," "Oh?," "Really?" Stay engaged.
2. Take time when appropriate to validate and clarify.

Let's look at some communication busters. These are sometimes consciously used to shut someone down, but very often they are subconscious, knee-jerk reactions because of our own insecurity or lack of awareness of our impact on others. This is why nurturing awareness is so important. Be sure to avoid the following:

1. Interrupting before the other person is finished talking.
2. Correcting what or how something has been said rather than hearing the bigger message that is being conveyed.
3. Using sarcasm or joking in a mean way.
4. Trying to fix the problem instead of just supporting the one speaking.
5. Using a superior, judgmental, angry, or bored tone of voice.
6. Droning on and on without regard to whether or not the other is interested.
7. Not listening.
8. Not answering a question.
9. Talking in circles without getting to the point.
10. Defensiveness.

What can we do to avoid the above reactions? We need to consider them in two ways:

First, how do we respond when someone does it to us?

Second, how can we be aware of our own communication-busting and change it?

Remember, in whatever situation you find yourself, you want to be conscious and aware of your thoughts, feelings, and actions. Only then can you be the most effective communicator possible. You are no longer a victim of the whims of others or blown about by their careless actions and words. You are thoughtful and aware. Change cannot happen until you are aware of what is going on and what you want to change.

One way to notice if *you* do these things is to pay attention to what people say in reaction to communicating with you. "You never listen." "You're always judging me." "Stop trying to fix me." Instead of being defensive, just validate what you hear them saying and apologize. It is so much easier than you think.

With all these techniques, remember that if you take a deep breath and detach yourself from the other person's possibly offensive delivery, it keeps you from getting sucked into negative emotions and reactiveness.

As soon as you catch yourself in one of the disruptive patterns, just stop. Then choose another way.

Delivering an Uncomfortable Message

Difficult or uncomfortable conversations are simply the price of doing business. When issues are confronted gently and directly, they are resolved more quickly and with fewer hard feelings. When you accept this, you will find your way further along the path to better productivity.

Yes, everyone has feelings that need to be respected and validated, but don't let that stop you from communicating things that need to be communicated.

If you want something to change, you have to do something about it.

We must learn to get over our fears and insecurities. Fear keeps us from addressing issues that need to be addressed. We are afraid of how the other person will respond or that it might cause more problems; we don't feel secure enough to handle someone else's strong emotions. All of these and many more are reasons why we don't confront issues. But the more we sweep them under the rug, the more they fester. *Nothing* gets better by being swept under the rug! It will manifest in some way sooner or later.

This is why it's *so* important to practice connecting to your source, developing a strong sense of self so that your fears are minimized and your judgmental thoughts are no longer prominent.

When you practice the 10 Essential Principles laid out in the last chapter, you lay the groundwork for things to get done. You clear the field of debris, so you can institute healthier communication practices unencumbered by fear, self-consciousness, or trigger points. You lay a secure foundation in your heart and mind, allowing a clear space for forgiveness and gratitude. You become more aware of what's going on in you and around you. You learn to take a deep breath and detach, knowing where the other person ends and you begin. While we are all connected on an energetic level, we have to keep clear emotional boundaries so that one person's emotional meltdown doesn't become your tar pit. This enables you to communicate your need without being put off by their emotional (or possibly unreasonable) response. You recognize that others have the same right to their emotions as you do, but just because they're turning on the drama doesn't mean you have to buy a ticket to the show.

By practicing mindfulness and establishing a meditation practice, you develop an ability to avoid getting caught up in the whirlwind of emotion and reactiveness, keeping you as still as the eye of the storm.

The beginning of wisdom
is to realize that, as
humans,
we know next to nothing.
Give up the need to be
right.
Give up your box.
Give up your judgment
and prejudice.
Practice love.
That's where we need to
begin and end.

Marianne Clyde

- marianneclyde.com

CHAPTER 6

Now You See It. Now You Don't!

It's nice to have a list of behaviors that you'd like to avoid and another list that you'd like to pursue. It's also great to have some principles to keep in mind to guide your steps. But how do you actually get set free? The bills still need to be paid; your spouse still has a differing opinion and has irritating habits that drive you nuts. The kids have their own lives but need to be transported to those various activities. Then there's homework to do, a house to clean, animals to take care of, not to mention a boss that needs to be satisfied or you're potentially out of a job. And then, of course, your spouse expects you to leave all your stress at the office and have a nice romantic dinner followed by a wonderfully fulfilling night of lovemaking. No problem.

The issue here seems to be that your brain is spinning, and you can't stop it long enough to get a grip. Perhaps you find yourself being an overly sensitive, often angry and resentful person who wants to quit because life is just too hard.

It's important that you begin to pay attention to patterns. Are you always angry? Can the smallest inconvenience or annoyance set you off? Does it take longer for you to calm down but you are triggered by smaller things?

Did you know that it's quite possible to be addicted to feelings and reactions? The process is pretty much the same as an addiction to an outside substance. Your body is filled with "receptors" that receive and respond to certain chemicals, whether it's alcohol, heroin, or a chemical released in your brain when you get angry or sad, or fall in love. You can be addicted to depression, anxiety, excitement, danger, or feeling offended.

A good way to see if you are addicted to a feeling is to examine your own experience. Is everyone else "an idiot?" Does "everybody" make you mad or seem to be mean or plotting against you? Are you fearful or anxious? If so, perhaps you are addicted to feeling like a victim.

The good news is that while it may not always feel like it, you actually do have control over these feelings. Nobody else can ever "make you" mad or afraid. The response comes from within you; therefore, you can change that response.

In some way, you get a payoff from feeling a certain way, even if it's negative, such as feeling like a victim or being anxious all the time. Perhaps it keeps you safe at home or justifies not taking responsibility. Maybe it keeps you from looking like the "bad guy" or from making difficult decisions.

If you want to be rid of a certain habit, you must first see what you are getting from that habit, so you can find a replacement. You may smoke or drink because you think it calms you. Well, until you decide on other ways to be calm, that will continue to be your "go-to" stress relief.

The key to being set free is to realize that the trap, or the chain that binds you, is actually connected to your thoughts about the behavior, emotion, or circumstances. And you can change your thoughts in an instant. When you are truly free and unbound inside, no person, thought, or thing will ever be able to hold you captive again.

Making changes in any area is difficult; but if your life is being complicated by habitual or addictive anger, it's time to take a tough look at where you are, why you are there, and where you want to go. Then you can begin to change.

Our emotions are connected to our beliefs. If you believe that in order to protect yourself, you must react in anger, not only does the anger need to go, but the belief needs to change.

The belief was formed by a strong emotion being seared into our cells by a possibly traumatic event or series of events. It might have been an atmosphere at home in which no one was heard unless they yelled and the angriest person "won." Anger may have originated in a sense of helplessness, loneliness, or unfairness.

Anxiety could be rooted in a child who was burdened with too much responsibility for his age. Or it could come from not being validated or heard, leaving a child to feel incompetent, always second guessing himself. Or it could simply be learned by observing an anxious parent.

The same goes for anything that is keeping you stuck: poor relationships that cause you grief at work, an inability to stop procrastinating, which keeps your boss on your back, a visceral reaction to certain types of people—the list goes on. The causes are as individual as the person's experience, but the way to get unstuck and move on is often the same.

This is not to minimize serious mental disorders or very difficult situations, and these suggestions are by no means intended to replace the need for therapy.

But the process for getting set free from destructive habits, addictive thinking that is interfering in your life, unfulfilling relationships, or unhealthy behavior patterns is relatively simple. And no one can do it for you. You are the one with all the power.

Often clients will come into my office saying things like they need to find a new job because their boss is a "psychopath," or that they will never be happy until their adult child apologizes, or that they can't stay in a marriage if their spouse doesn't stop being so inconsiderate. Some say things like, "I'll never find any peace as long as my son continues to pursue behaviors that I don't approve of."

Well, I find that very sad. Because what each of those people is saying to me is this: "I have no control over my life, and I am choosing to let someone else's behavior, belief system, or behavior patterns govern the way I feel and how I live my life."

Of course that is their choice. But it would be much more freeing and empowering to learn to control your feelings and choose your thought patterns and beliefs so that you can live the life of joy and freedom that you were created to live. Freedom comes from within and manifests outwardly, not the other way around. And I am going to show you how you can be free.

Blast Through What's Keeping You Stuck! Identify the Emotion

The first thing to do if you are feeling stuck is to identify the emotion and the belief or thought pattern that is keeping you there. This can have nothing to do with anyone else. It cannot require an apology or someone to change. This only has to do with you and your reaction.

We will be looking at things like *how you feel* when your wife snaps at you, rather than *why* your wife snaps at you. You'll focus on *how you feel* before you reach for that extra piece of cake, rather than what kind of diet you might want to begin. We'll address *how you feel* when your boss totally disregards your personal needs when she requires you to stay late, rather than why "she's such a bitch." This is all about you. Not about them. You can only change you. You might even be surprised at how effective changing yourself can be! *Other people may quite possibly begin to respond to you differently after you have made the changes in your thoughts.*

Identify the Physical Sensations

Once you identify the feeling, such as anger, sit for a minute and mentally scan your body for associated feelings. What happens in your body when your boss acts that way or when you get a phone call in the middle of the night? What does that anxiety feel like as it surges through your body? Does it create pressure in your chest? Is there tightness in your throat? Does your head feel as if there is a clamp around it? Is your stomach doing flips? Do you feel tension in your muscles? Prickly feeling in your fingertips?

We associate a physical sensation to an emotional feeling. We don't intellectualize or analyze why we feel a certain way. It doesn't have to make sense. We are going to look into your past for the first time you felt like this.

We spend so much time in our heads trying to figure out why things are happening, and we try to stop it by changing our behavior. The truth is the belief was branded into your body with a strong emotion. It happened in the feeling realm, not in the thinking realm. The body has its own intellect and that's where it needs to be changed.

When you were a child, you didn't think about why daddy left. You just watched him go; it felt like a sucker punch, and you believed you did something wrong. The feeling came first. The feeling takes you to the belief, not the other way around. But as you become an adult, the thoughts and feelings work together to send out energy that communicates to others, "People leave me because there's something wrong with me." So in order to protect yourself from getting hurt, maybe you push them away first with anger, or sabotage the relationship, or project onto others the hate you feel toward yourself. Every situation is different, but we do things and act the way we do for a reason, and it's usually subconscious. In order to change it, we must bring it onto the conscious level, so that it no longer haunts us in the shadows. When it is brought to light, you find that the big monster that you've been fighting is a scared and lonely child who didn't really understand what was going on and inadvertently created beliefs around an incident that became a self-fulfilling prophecy in your life.

It's time to take your life back and let the past be in the past!

Find Where it Started

After you've identified the emotion and the physical feeling that goes with it, just take some deep breaths, relax, and let your mind drift back as far as you can go. You will be looking for the first time you felt this way. Nine times out of 10 it's pretty early in childhood. One client talks about finding her healing from as far back as the womb.

This woman battled with bulimia for 20 years, which included six hospitalizations, multiple therapists, and many different food control plans. She says I helped her link her eating disorder to feelings of "intense deprivation" ingrained in her while she was still in the womb. As it turned out, her mother dieted while she was pregnant. She also drank and smoked. "While I was in the womb, I was deprived of food and oxygen," she said.

As an adult, this client felt that she "would die" if she did not binge and purge. "We found the belief that was triggering my behavior and replaced it with truth. Once that happened, I stopped bingeing and purging. The desire is completely gone—100%," she says.

I have heard similar things from clients dealing with anger. As a child, one woman apparently saw someone shoot a beloved family member, and she had buried the fear and horror. But after examining the situation from a place of remembering the feeling, she was able to see that the anger had held her captive all those years, and was able to say, "I don't feel it anymore." "Don't feel what anymore?" I asked. "The anger," she said. "It's just gone." She was able to go back, find the memory associated with the anger, and change the belief that held her prisoner for so long.

Let's talk about how to find and change the belief that's holding you captive. When you've got such emotionally exhausting programs running in the background of your mind, under the surface of conscious thought, it takes an incredible amount of energy to do just about anything. So of course it will interfere with your productivity.

It's just impossible for you to be completely present in the moment with chaos going on under the surface.

Changing Your Beliefs

After you have identified the emotion, located the feeling in your body, and traced the feeling back to a particular memory or series of memories, now you need to try to remember what was going on and ask yourself what you believed in that moment. Don't get too caught up in the details since they can morph over the years, as any set of siblings remembering the exact same incident totally differently will clearly tell you.

I would say in *most* cases the details don't really matter. What matters is how you felt, what you believed because of how you felt, and then moving on to create a new belief. You remember something in a certain way, eliciting lots of emotion and creating beliefs that have manipulated your world for a long time. That's the part I'm interested in. I want to see you feel better and get unstuck from whatever is keeping you down.

There are many books written about memories, but I particularly like one called *Mistakes Were Made (but not by me)* by Carol Tavris and Elliott Aronson. An interesting read about how memory actually works, it talks about how we each create memories in which we look good. We remember things from a very personal perspective, which often gets mingled with bits of truth, making it difficult to discern exactly what really happened. The main focus is actually how you felt and what you believed as a child. You might find that what you believed and have held onto all these years is not true anymore. Yes, you might have been helpless then. You might have been devastated and felt unloved. You might have wanted to disappear and be invisible. But that's not working for you anymore, so you have to change the belief. Once you change the belief, the feelings will follow.

Having said that, when you have identified the belief, close your eyes and ask the wisdom that created the universe—the truth that dwells in you—to reveal itself in this case. For example, if you believed you were unlovable or incompetent, or that you didn't matter or couldn't trust anyone, simply invite the truth into the memory where you felt vulnerable. Invite the truth to speak or reveal itself to the belief that you are unlovable and just let it come. It might come in a thought, vision, or feeling. It might come in a sentence or in an aroma, releasing you from the anguish. Just allow all your senses to be available to the truth, and you will know that you are loved or important or capable in that moment.

As the tension, anger, or loneliness dissipates, just sit and marinate in that feeling and energy for a few minutes until you feel ready, then open your eyes. Now you can apply that feeling to the reactiveness when your wife snaps at you or your boss doesn't agree to your request. You are no longer hooked into a triggered reaction. You are free to engage in a thoughtful response based on new information.

There are many thirsty
souls that you pass by
each day.
Make sure your emotional
bucket is full.
They may have no place
else to drink.
Marianne Clyde

CHAPTER 7

Establishing a Firm Foundation for Change

You may be wondering how meditation fits into a book about making your business more productive and profitable. Easy. Being successful on or off the job is all about focus and how you use your energy. It's about how well you communicate and manage your time, and how you get along with others. How flexible are you? Do you adapt well to change? Do you take responsibility for what you say and do? Are you able to think outside the box? How well do you maintain your physical and mental well-being so that you can show up at work with lots of energy, ready to hit the ground running?

Yes, of course it also has to do with how well you know your job and perform the tasks required of you. Absolutely it's about being qualified and having a certain skill set and/or degree. But it's important to know that even though skills, talent, and certain qualifications play an important role, these are generally secondary to the things mentioned in the previous paragraph. It is a rare organization that will keep you employed if you continue to overuse your sick leave, have explosive anger outbursts, or refuse to communicate with your coworkers in a productive way. An employer whose main goal is to make a profit is unlikely to let you continue on an unproductive path by letting your personal problems distract you from your focus at work for an extended period.

Every business owner wants his company to operate like a well-oiled machine. If there are broken parts or programs running that can't communicate with each other, he is going to have to discard the non-working parts and get new ones. This is not personal. It's business.

Meditation is like oil for the machine. It keeps things running without friction and helps all the different parts read the same page of music, even though they may be playing different instruments.

Most people over the course of their day are dancing as fast as they can. They work hard to get everything done on their to-do list—getting the kids to school and after-school activities; planning dinner; processing how to resolve that disagreement they had with the neighbor; and getting to work in time for the staff meeting. And that's just a normal load.

Imagine all of these programs running in your head while simultaneously there's a trauma from your past that you've really never dealt with. What if your wife died of cancer last year and your dad is in the hospital from a recent heart attack? What if, on top of that, or should we say, underneath all that, your childhood was one of neglect and abuse, so there is a program running underneath all of the primary and secondary stressors that says you are unworthy and un-loveable?

And at the same time, you are expected to be efficient at work and producing ever-better results? This may sound extreme, but it's a very common scenario. The details may change, but the variety of problems and stressors that find their way into each of our lives is about the same. How do we stay sane in the midst of all the chaos?

Ah, yes. That brings us back to the purpose of meditation. It's like a defragmentation service for your brain. When your computer has too many programs running at the same time, it uses up its brain space. The same goes for you. It's important to delete the programs that are no longer necessary, heal up the programs that are necessary but broken, and maintain optimum efficiency by using the least amount of energy. After all, you need energy left at the end of the day to enjoy your friends and family and do the things that you love. Meditation needs to be done regularly to ensure optimal health and maximum performance.

When you are dragged down by issues from your past, you cannot give your full attention and energy to the present moment. It's impossible to be fully present with your loved ones or even at your job when your subconscious is running fear, anger, resentment, or insecurity in the background.

Not too long ago, a woman whom I was coaching agreed that she has never been able to give herself completely to her partner emotionally because of the shame and anger from her past. We must become aware of our blockages to productivity, joy, and love so that we can move beyond them. It's very sad when we feel condemned by ourselves and others because we feel like we *should* be able to love our partner completely, but something deep down inside of us just feels stuck. This is not the place for condemnation; it's an opportunity for healing.

Once we recognize that, it is important to develop a regular habit of being still and listening—focusing on this present moment and your connection to all that is. You need to get comfortable and familiar with the one who created you and loves you more that you could ever even imagine. You need to get to know your true identity. Meditation allows all of this.

Meditation can be done in many ways. The important thing is that you find a method that works for you, and do it. I recommend 20 minutes twice a day. Some people do more, some less, but the main point is to begin. You can do guided meditation, as I have done from time to time, or you can do it on your own.

I have considerable experience in different kinds of meditation. I have studied Transcendental Meditation, Zazen, Primordial Sound, and Japa as well as learned about early Christian mystics and their meditation practices. I have read in the Bible the many verses about meditating on God's law and immersing ourselves in Him and His teachings.

From my research of varied practices, I have learned what seems to be a theme: Connecting with the source of life, the energy that moves through all things, the universal mind, becoming so familiar that it makes our way straight. "Be still," we are told.

This can be done in many ways. Choose a time and place where you won't be disturbed. You may use a timer if you like, but it is best if the chime is soft and gentle.

When I first started meditating over 20 years ago, I would set the timer on the microwave for 10 minutes. It's amazing how long 10 minutes can feel when you are used to being constantly busy, but hang in there. It will get easier.

Many people are so overwhelmed with "yet one more obligation" when I suggest they start a practice, so keep in mind this is not to overwhelm you; it's to help you get things in order. Sometimes if all you have is a couple of minutes in the shower to close your eyes and take a few deep breaths, then begin with that every day. You are probably going to shower anyway, so it shouldn't add stress. I have also recommended to people who are on the run all the time just to take a few deep, mindful breaths at each stoplight.

Generally, I suggest that you start with a quiet place where you can be undisturbed and sit comfortably. Creating a habit around the place and time can put a frame of structure around your practice that can make it easier to remember and follow through.

Once you are sitting comfortably, set your timer or just glance at the clock and determine the amount of time you plan to spend. Love yourself enough to do this. You deserve this time, and it will begin to make things less stressful for you and keep you calmer and healthier.

Choose a thought on which your mind can rest. Perhaps it is just focusing on the sensations around your breath: a gentle inhale and exhale, noticing how the air feels entering your nostrils and leaving through your nose or mouth. Feel your diaphragm rise and fall. And just do this for the allotted time.

A mindfulness-based meditation can be focused on one body part at a time, starting with the top of your head, feeling the sensations there for a few seconds, then moving to your eyes, ears, nose, lips, and so on, down to your toes. Rest your attention gently and just observe—do not judge. Feel the sensation of sitting on the chair or resting your arms and hands in your lap. Observe the stress leave your body.

I recommend closing your eyes because it shuts out extra stimulation and makes it easier to drop into a slower brain wave pattern, relaxing you. If you do not feel comfortable closing your eyes, you can gently rest your gaze a few feet ahead of you on the floor, keeping your gaze relaxed and unfocused.

Perhaps you'd have an easier time focusing if you had a mantra to repeat over and over in your head. Some types of training will assign you a mantra, or you can choose your own. I like "I AM" as a mantra, reminding me of my oneness with God and His perfect state of being. You can also use *ahum* ("I am" in Sanskrit) or *om*, focusing on the vibrational quality of the letters. Many people just use any name for God such as Yahweh or Jehovah. Some people prefer to choose an emotion or feeling such as love, joy, compassion, or peace as the object of their attention.

Whatever you choose, gently repeat that mantra silently, or aloud if you like, for the duration of your allotted meditation time, be it two minutes or an hour.

You will have thoughts. That may surprise you, but don't let it bother you. Your brain is just doing what it's designed to do. When extraneous thoughts come, quietly bring your focus back to the breath or the mantra. You are quieting your mind. You are retraining your thought processes to be still and content. You are actually rewiring the brain.

When a pond is still, it is much easier to see the reflection of nature. When your mind is still, it is easier to see the reflection of your true self and listen to the still small voice within you that knows all things. Most of the time we are too busy to hear it. But when we take time to listen and let our thoughts get organized, we can be much calmer as we approach the day.

When we are anxious and stressed, our brainwaves move pretty fast, and stress hormones are constantly released into our bodies. Unchecked levels of cortisol can cause anxiety and depression, weight gain, high blood pressure, muscle weakness, fatigue, and insomnia.

Besides this, constantly high levels of adrenalin can cause arrhythmia, acid reflux, and panic disorders. So it's obviously very important to keep these under control, which is what meditation can help you do.

The point is not to analyze if you are doing it right, because just doing it in the best way you can brings many benefits. Sitting down and slowing your thoughts and heart rate once or twice a day means that you are doing it right. You can sometimes begin to notice benefits in a very short period of time. Here's a story that demonstrates this very well.

The owner of a struggling tire business, Thomas is a family guy with a beautiful wife and four amazing kids. He knows how to get stuff done. He motivates his employees, has a great sense of humor, and is really fun to be around. But there was a time when, every now and then, Thomas exploded, and it wasn't pretty. He yelled and was abusive to his workers, and that anger carried over to his home life. Without any predictable markers around his anger, it was difficult to maneuver around him because you never really knew what would set him off. His employees and his family found themselves walking on eggshells because one thing was certain: several times a week, he blew his top when something didn't go his way.

One day during a routine business deal, a vendor accused him of something he didn't do, which might have soured the deal. His wife held her breath, waiting for his explosion. He turned to her and said, "I am going to need to consult my attorney about this." He told the vendor that the accusation was false and he would get back to him. He spent the next two or three hours consulting with his attorney, finding proof that the accusation was not true, and asked the attorney to write a letter affirming his innocence and to attach the proof. The attorney sent the information to the vendor via email, so that the business transaction could continue.

During that time, Thomas never raised his voice or let out any vile accusations. He never denigrated the vendor. There was no puffing, panting, or growling. He simply said, "Well, that's not true, and I'll show you." He went about the business of seeking out proof in a calm, methodical way while his wife stood by with her mouth open saying to him, "What did you do with my husband?"

The problem was resolved in a couple of hours, and business went on as usual. What happened to Thomas? Why didn't he react in his typical way?

As it turns out, a few weeks before, Thomas started a haphazard meditation practice. He didn't have time, he said, to sit for 20 or 30 minutes twice a day, like I generally recommend. But he did have time occasionally for about five minutes. He did have time to close his eyes and take a few deep breaths when he pulled his truck up to a stoplight. He had learned to take a breath before answering any question or reacting to any situation.

And it worked. He changed his reactivity into Zentivity. He got the results he wanted with a small practice of quieting his mind throughout the day. Instead of losing a deal over the thoughtless words of another businessman—who surely would have dropped the deal if Thomas had his typical reaction, his wife witnessed what she considered a miracle. He had responded thoughtfully. She wasn't embarrassed to be with him, as had happened so many times previously, and they got the deal. She had seen many deals lost in the past because of her husband's explosive anger and was flabbergasted to see the effectiveness of just making a few small changes by laying a foundation of calm, which grounded him and gave him a strong surface from which to rebound when he felt like he was knocked down.

Because he did this, his business experienced the results of his Zentivity: a calm inner foundation that led to more productive results.

Quick helps for anxiety:

1. Long slow deep breath.

2. Realize that it's your body's way of telling you it thinks you might be in danger. (Just thank your body, and tell it you're ok.)

3. You learned this reaction in childhood when you were powerless.
(You have better coping skills now; remind yourself of that.)

4. When the thoughts start spinning, stop them and replace them with positive, powerful thoughts like: I can do this.

5. If you treat anxiety like the enemy, it will persist. If you just let it be and move on, you will see how powerful you really are.

Marianne Clyde, LMFT

- marianneclyde.com

CHAPTER 8

Implementing Healthy Practices in the Workplace

When I asked business owners and executives what they do to increase productivity and make their employees happier, by far the most common response was to show recognition to employees for a job well done. And financial reward was the most frequent way that this is done.

Depending on the type of business, financial benefits were given by way of bonuses, profit sharing, perks such as company cars, discounts on products manufactured by the company, percentage of sales, and parties.

As important and effective as financial compensation has proven to be, other kinds of personal recognition came in as a close second as the most used type of instrument to enhance employee satisfaction. Things like random compliments or "catching them doing something well," demonstrating personal interest in the employee by taking time to know their birthdays, anniversaries, families, and personal situations. Understanding as much as possible that personal crises do arise from time to time and allowing for flexibility for family emergencies has evoked employee appreciation for these business owners.

Also important is the need for clear communication that includes regular open staff meetings where employee input is recognized and valued, and where there is no separation due to secrecy between employees and management. A frequent complaint and reason for lack of productivity was unclear communication from management, or that different employees were held to different standards of performance. And almost each person that I spoke to mentioned the importance of listening to employees. Don't turn a deaf ear; allow all constructive feedback. It's important to hear what employees are saying, even if you don't agree with them. When you hear the same complaint over and over, there is probably something to it. If you want to retain your employees, they need to feel heard. Open communication and consistency is vital.

All these things are easier to do, if you, as an employer or manager, are calm and self-confident. You will find yourself more generous and less reactive, as well as wiser and calmer, yet still expecting everyone's best. People often rise to an expectation that is clearly put forth. They also respond when they feel validated.

Employers find that of particular interest to their employees is the ability for their input to be factored significantly in decision-making. Some employers that I spoke to allow decisions to be made by teams of employees instead of management. And sometimes surveys were given to employees, and management took specific action based on those recommendations. Feeling valued, important, and as a significant part of the company's mechanism seems to bring out better retention and decreased use of sick days.

Trust extended to employees through increased responsibility, where goals are clearly presented with regular accountability meetings, encourages commitment and engagement. When management clearly and regularly communicates expectations and goals, employees tend to be more productive. There appears to be more motivation to accomplish tasks at hand when employees are given clear direction, and allowed to assume responsibility with minimal micromanagement.

With 66% percent of employees in the United States claiming

that they are disengaged in their jobs, employers need to find a way to get their people involved, invested, and even excited about coming to work. How can we expect them to be engaged when work is not engaging? Or when they are not valued or their input doesn't make a difference? People are social animals and thrive with a sense of community, but they tend to wither away when they are isolated. They need to know that they matter and that the community needs them and values them.

People also thrive on healthy competition. For example, I heard Colonel Edward L. Hubbard, a Vietnam War POW, speak at a gathering. Surviving on about 300–400 calories a day, he and the other prisoners were confined to cells that measured about five square feet. He says in his book, *Escape from the Box: The Wonder of Human Potential*, that you don't really appreciate how much we need competition in our lives until you begin to feel completely unproductive. "Competition gives your life direction," he says, "so you know which way to go when you get up each day." He adds, "Competition is the force that makes your life productive. When life ceases to be productive, what results is the most empty and worthless feeling on earth. You can never appreciate the value of competition until it is removed from your life."

He and his fellow prisoners were barely surviving on a meager diet under the watchful eyes of harsh and uncaring captors. They had to figure out for themselves how to find meaning and a reason to survive. So they created daily exercise goals, ultimately creating competitions between each other and themselves, pushing them far beyond the point their minds could ever conceive. They competed in push-ups, sit-ups, and jump rope. This competitive atmosphere created purpose and a reason to exist. Their achievements were extraordinary. One thousand push-ups before breakfast! Two thousand sit-ups! And 3,640 consecutive jumps with the jump rope. This is what he could do by the time he was released from prison. It's amazing what a little determination and competition can do.

Now I am not suggesting that you institute a jump rope

competition at your place of business, but providing opportunities within the workplace environment to compete in a healthy way for the health and benefit of the whole team can be done in a variety of ways.

Many business owners and executives affirm how important it is to receive personal recognition. Validation for a job well done can enhance performance. Employees need to feel engaged and responsible, but not trapped. This kind of validation might include opportunities for employees to receive some sort of benefit for their commitment and hard work. Not every company can offer a promotion to their employees when they perform well, but many offer some kind of reward, validation, bonus and/or recognition to people who have performed above company standards in their attitude and behavior. And all of them recognized the importance of this. Something as small as a gift card for a coffee shop or a massage, while not very expensive, can offer a message that the employees are appreciated. It always amazes me how far some people will go just for a small bit of recognition. All of the leaders that I spoke to noticed an increase in productivity and satisfaction level of the employees when these kinds of policies were implemented.

One company I know of has a "Five-a-Day" competition to encourage employees to eat healthy by getting five fruits and vegetables a day. Another company gave their employees Fitbits as Christmas gifts, encouraging them to get to 10,000 steps a day. Other types of creative ideas for healthy perks include such things as a gym in the building, massages, yoga classes, or a cafeteria with inexpensive healthy food choices. When going to work is stimulating and fun, it makes the stress of deadlines and production demands easier to handle.

Another thing noted as helpful to increasing productivity was being organized and prepared. Some offices offer regular training. When I lived in Tokyo, one of the partners at PricewaterhouseCoopers encouraged their employees to be involved in humanitarian efforts and asked me to speak at their regular staff meeting about my travels around the globe, helping people in developing countries overcome trauma. This kind of outside-the-box thinking encourages employees to see themselves as able to contribute to the larger community in a different, highly impactful way. This helped train his employees in the art of compassion, empathy, and life balance, which can then be translated to the work setting.

A car dealership owner emphasized to me how important it is for him to maintain his sense of humor and steady demeanor, as it encourages his employees to feel secure. The owner of a successful plumbing business said that empathy goes a long way as well—his door is always open to his employees.

It's not always what you do specifically, but who you are as a person that can be inspirational. If your employees see you—the top person—being self-aware and taking responsibility for your own emotions and responses, chances are they will be more likely to follow suit.

Simply by being centered enough to be aware of what's going on with your staff, you can nip problems in the bud, mitigating potential disasters and taking the risk to confront problematic behavior.

Even Brenda, an employee at a local establishment, deserved respect and needed validation despite the fact that she drove everyone around her crazy. She was often fun to be around, but she could turn on a dime and take your head off. She had the ambition to rise in the company and didn't mind working the less-desirable hours, but her erratic behavior caused her boss to think about letting her go. The other employees were starting to complain, and once in a while, her employer noticed the looks that she got from a customer whom she snapped at.

He decided to call her into his office to see what was going on. He discovered that her mother had died just a few months before, her child was in trouble at school, and the teacher suggested he needed testing. Her husband was in Iraq and she found herself constantly on edge. She felt like a single mom, trying to make ends meet.

Her boss expressed empathy but also clearly told her how her erratic behavior was affecting the customers and other employees. She had no idea. She had never considered how to deal with her fears, anxiety, and grief in a healthier way. It turned out that his simple expression of empathy—giving her an opportunity to talk and get her troubles off her chest, was what she needed. She agreed to be more self-aware and take responsibility for her behavior. That one talk with her boss made a big difference, and she practically changed overnight. It's amazing how a little face time and genuine concern can shine a light on someone's blind spot, leading to a change in behavior.

Confrontation has gotten a bad rap. We try to avoid confrontation at all costs; but the truth is, when you take the time to confront a problem or an issue that you've been avoiding, doing it in a respectful, empathetic way, it can breed intimacy in a relationship and stimulate a behavior change. When confronted with anger and accusation, the accused automatically gets defensive and digs her heels in—and the situation gets worse almost every time. A little compassion and patience goes a long way.

In the next chapter we will look at ways that management can help employees live a Zentivity lifestyle. Staying grounded, being aware of your triggers, and taking responsibility for handling them effectively allows you to live a principled life from your true identity, creating and communicating effectively, which attracts abundance to you as you are more productive. You can truly be a powerful leader and not a micromanaging task master.

PART THREE
Productivity

Drama.
It's like quicksand.
Don't let it suck you in.

Marianne Clyde

CHAPTER 9

Happy Employees, Happy Bottom Line

Happy employees that feel valued and heard are productive employees. People who are recognized for their contribution and given space and opportunity to make decisions so they can feel empowered and free to be themselves take responsibility seriously. Taking more ownership in the company's results, employees are given regular feedback, positive as well as constructive, offering a chance for them to give feedback as well. These employees feel as though they are making a difference and that the company wouldn't be the same without them, leading to better retention, minimal turnover, and a less disgruntled workforce.

This was well-illustrated by a government agency head who led a demoralized, unproductive agency toward vibrancy and productivity by encouraging senior and middle managers to hear, consider, and discuss employee concerns. Then, as decisions were made about employee feedback, results were monitored and reviewed on a monthly basis, tracking their impact. He said, "Every quantifiable indicator improved rapidly." Everyone could see the results, which gave new confidence to the decision-making process within the agency. It clearly paid for him to create an environment where employees were given the freedom and opportunity to discuss their concerns, knowing they would be heard and validated.

The owner of a popular and thriving printing business says that whenever she is not confident of a solution, she immediately calls in professional help and counsel. What is so wise about this is the recognition that the business owner can't do everything. She can't know everything. She uses the multitude of skills that she has, but when she doesn't know, she admits it and calls in professional help to consult or train. One shortcoming of many businesses is the unwillingness of management to admit when they need outside help. When you allow other professionals to assist you, it takes the pressure off so that you can do what you do well, while the consultant does what he or she does well.

So What Does All This Mean?

How can we distill all this information into a plan of action for you to help your company to achieve Zentivity? How can your employees experience that calm place from where productivity grows? The simple answer is that it all begins with you. If you are a manager, business owner, or executive, your own personal mental health and stability set a precedent at your place of business. Others are watching you and learning from you what is acceptable behavior. If you are reactive, angry, and lack self-control, it sends the message that this type of atmosphere is not only okay, but may be acceptable and expected. Others will follow suit.

If, on the other hand, you have developed your own practice of stillness, and you live in a calm, self-assured place within yourself, you send out energy that makes you more approachable. Employees feel safer in approaching you because they know you will not bark at them or invalidate them for having an opinion or a personal need. It puts you in a position, by reason of your personal demeanor, not only to offer helpful options, but to ask them to consider changing their behavior in certain ways. Meditation has worked for you;

perhaps it will work for them. Taking personal responsibility for your feelings makes you more effective with people; maybe it would have the same effect in their lives. Acknowledging your triggers and responding appropriately has benefitted you, so you are in a position to suggest that it might also work for them. This makes you not only more authentic and real, it gives you a natural air of authority from which they can learn and grow. You certainly can't legislate peace or even mental health, but you can model it and let your employees know that while it's understandable that personal issues and life circumstances can threaten to throw you off balance, there are options to being out of control. There are tangible, easy practices that you can model and expect from your people. These practices and habits not only instill a sense of calm well-being, but create better productivity and profits for your company.

Success Stories

Here are some real-life examples demonstrating how these teachings have worked for people just like you, and how it has made a difference in their businesses.

When I started working with Mark, the head of the maintenance department in a mid-sized corporation, he said "distraction" was the word of the hour. His personal life and his business life bled into each other. He said there was a "cloud over everything," and he just couldn't function. He was dealing with anxiety that caused obsessive thinking and alcohol addiction.

His day was spent focusing on his perceived faults, women, and his addiction. He said that by 1:00 p.m. each day, his focus on the task at hand diminished, and his attention turned to 5:00 p.m., when he could get out of there and drink. So for the entire afternoon, he was mentally "not there." He admits, "There was no productivity whatsoever."

Through our work together, he learned that the way he spent his evenings and how he woke up each morning set the tone for how his day went. So he started a practice of having a proactive morning conversation with himself. He began to ask, "Where am I, and what am I trying to do?" After answering those questions, he says, "OK, let's make some money today!" which focuses him in the direction of work.

He used to be completely overwhelmed with obsessive thoughts, believing that he had no choice but to let them run rampant in his mind. After learning that he had a choice about which thoughts to think, he began to notice when the onslaught of thoughts began to form, and he was able to stop them.

Then, he would address one thought at a time. He understood that he could control his thinking if he became aware of what was happening. He determined if a thought was a priority. If it wasn't, he replaced it with a productive one, asking, "What's one thing I can do right now to address the task at hand?" Then he addressed the next thought and the next, until he controlled all of them, tossing out the low-priority ones that caused him to feel overwhelmed and choosing a productive thought and action, learning to refocus on work.

Mark realized that his attitude and those of everyone around him depended on his ability to control his thoughts and his reactions. He now asserts, "A positive, healthy mindset and thought process is absolutely vital to the well-being of the company. My thinking affects how I respond to staff and how they feel about themselves. My responses to their needs and questions determine how efficiently something gets done. If I am dismissive and removed from them and react badly, it only prolongs the problem."

Mark remembers at one time planning huge events worth hundreds of thousands of dollars for a general manager who didn't even know his name. "This guy trusted me with large amounts of money and responsibility, and there was never any acknowledgement of a job well done." He was just a cog in a wheel to that general manager, and company morale was terrible.

Knowing how it feels not to be validated or acknowledged, Mark, now recovering from his addictions, recognizes the need to personally know everyone in the company, to encourage managers to know the people they manage by name, to know things about their families and their personal situations, and engage with them on a regular basis. Everyone must feel important and acknowledged. His company makes an effort to recognize employees for excellent work. They set regular goals, develop attainable budgets, and give bonuses to instill productivity. "Knowing who they are is a recipe for success," he says. "The power of knowing an employee's name goes *so* far." He stresses how knowing each employee and his or her needs and preferences can determine how you speak to them so that they feel validated and understood. He has found that blanket statements and reactions don't work the same with everyone. Knowing what works for each individual and using his communication skills to be efficiently productive has worked for him. And his employees are happier and more responsive, and thus more productive.

He likes the idea, when possible, of giving employees aggressive goals to be accomplished within a certain amount of time, but he lets the employees figure out how best to do that. If it can be done in three days and the employee spends the other two golfing, so be it. If it can be done from home, great. If they need to spend the time in the office to accomplish their tasks, then they may do that. He likes the recognition of individual preferences and skills within the framework of clear communication of expectations, rewards, and consequences.

Mark thinks the secret is starting your day well, taking time out when you need to clear your head with a breathing exercise or meditation, taking control of your thoughts, knowing your staff well, giving them the latitude to be themselves, and of course, communicating clearly and respectfully. He stands in awe as this handful of principles makes all the difference in the productivity in his business.

Bonnie, on the other hand, owns a popular restaurant chain that is known for its family-friendly atmosphere and variety of fun activities. While she has always taken pride in her ability to project an inner calm, she admits that often she felt chaotic and stressed inside. After beginning a meditation practice, she still projects an outward manifestation of calm, but inside, she is now less stressed and more balanced. Bonnie is better able to take the "right steps for the right reasons while being more patient and focused." Her place of business is experiencing a wide range of changes. She is selling the business and recently replaced senior management. By learning to engage in a regular meditation practice and more mindful outlook, she has learned what to allow, what to leave behind, and what losses she needs to accept.

By doing these things, she finds that she can carve out space to stop, think, consider, engage, and breathe as needed. She says that she can embrace this "rewarding burden of leadership, while remaining effective in the face of challenges with a clear internal voice." She says that she is more calm and balanced because "inside, I've changed."

"Owners need to lead," she says. And the people around her respond better when she leads with this balanced, straightforward approach.

Ted, a former client, says that the most important thing he learned from our work together was the realization about the amount of crossover between his personal life and his business. He owns a thriving shop with his wife, but he never realized how resolving business issues in a calm, thoughtful way had a powerful impact on his marriage and vice versa. He realized that many of their conflicts were over employee issues and business decisions. Now, because they have learned to address these issues when they first appear, rather that sweeping them under the rug, they've seen a big change at home and at the shop.

They have seen a direct impact on productivity in the way they address difficulties with employees in a timely manner—they don't let them fester. When issues are not addressed with clear communication of expectations, employees feel annoyed and begin to act out in ways that affect productivity. Ted and Hannah have implemented clear strategies about their employee expectations, provide them with the support needed to accomplish their tasks, and communicate the consequences if those tasks aren't completed.

Sometimes employees or managers need support to overcome personal issues that an employer is not qualified to give. That's why Ted supports things such as staff health savings accounts. He recognizes that he and Hannah need support and resources to help them through rough times. The main message he thinks they need to hear is: "You are not alone."

Because of their more "centered" approach to personal and business issues, Ted says that they recently weathered a financial crisis—which previously would have stressed them and their employees—with ease and grace, and they just experienced their top-grossing month ever.

He uses the tools of self-examination to manage stress as well as to find peace and the courage to do what he needs to do, even if it's difficult.

Today, I want to be out
of my mind.
Out from under
conditioned responses.
Out from under false or
man-made assumptions.
Out from under the
opinions of others.
Not bound by fear, or
irritations, or perceived
limitations.
I want to be fully aware
that this world is a
temporary experience
in an everlasting pool of
peace and love and joy.
My only job is to leave
some of that peace and
love and joy when I go.

Marianne Clyde

- marianneclyde.com

CHAPTER 10

Achieving Zentivity

Zentivity

A peaceful, calm environment in which employees are
actively engaged in the creative and productive process,
taking ownership in the process and results of their
work. End result: Companies make more money due
to better employee retention and cooperation.

While achieving Zentivity is a goal and a destination, it is also
the journey. It's a way of doing things and a state of being. It doesn't
mean that we are eliminating problems, conflicts, or pressures. Those
things are a natural outgrowth of a productive environment teeming
with different personality types, creative ideas, gifts, and talents.

It does mean, however, that your company will work more like
a well-oiled machine that gets regular tune-ups and uses only the
best parts available. Whether you run a law office or a plumbing
company, a big corporation or a family-run business, a factory or a
marketplace, as long as each person takes responsibility for *his or her*
role in the world, the effect that *he or she* has on others, the power
that *the individual* brings to the table in order to inspire change,
you will find that even though things are busily humming, they
are not chaotic. Even though problems arise, they will not trip you

up. Despite the fact that everyone has a differing opinion or way of doing things, communication is clear, direct, and respectful so that differences are resolved without throwing anyone under the bus, and everyone is invested in a positive outcome.

A top salesman in a well-known insurance company, Gary describes himself as "an extremely slow learner." He says as long as he can remember, he has struggled with "turning the squirrel cage off." He has always had difficulty slowing down enough to meditate, but he said, "You know what? I did it and it works!" He had witnessed a coworker seriously get into mindfulness and was amazed at her total transformation: her attitude, responses, and courageous and healthy decisions. She realized that she is only responsible for her own feelings and responses, not the volatile and angry responses of other people.

Gary used to act on his impulses but claims he is less apt to do that now. In the past, when a crisis happened, his mind immediately went into panic mode: "My life is screwed! This is the end of the world as we know it!" Now he is better able to take those thoughts less seriously. He has learned to pause and respond in a more collected, healthy way. He recognizes his feelings, and sometimes his first reaction to a difficult situation is still terror, but as he takes the time to detach and take a breath, he can present a calm demeanor for those in his department, and think more clearly to create a plan and work it, while being much less negative and fearful.

Clearly impacting his productivity, he is currently juggling several big clients. This kind of pressure used to paralyze him, and he could spend the whole day just frittering away the time without accomplishing anything. Now, with his ability to "stop the spinning squirrel cage" in his brain, he finds it easier to identify a place to start, make a plan, and chip away at it, one step at a time.

He has learned that "feelings are not facts" and is better able to see the scared child inside someone who is blustering and being reactive and hateful, and have more empathy for that person. He says that if he had reacted to the myriad of stressors in this past year in the same reactive, destructive way that he used to, he probably wouldn't be employed. Instead, he had his best financial year ever!

Remember Jim and Anna?

They let the moods and actions of each other and those around them determine their level of happiness and sense of well-being. When you are connected to your source and you realize deep down that you are one with that, you will find that nothing need overwhelm you or throw you off balance. It gives you a steadiness and assurance that regardless of what comes your way, you have choices in how to handle it. You understand that no matter what happens in your life, you are totally acceptable, loveable, and valuable. That doesn't change, indeed it *cannot* change just because something shocking, surprising, disappointing, or even devastating occurred in your world.

We learn to observe with curiosity and wonder. If Jim and Anna were more aware of their own feelings and could see beyond their own needs and expectations to those of each other, they might have had a conversation about what was actually going on, what was causing it, and how they could change it. As it was, they felt sad and powerless to change things.

On the other hand, the business owners and leaders in this book—those who learned and implemented the 10 Essential Principles—found that the communication techniques and mindfulness strategies identified where they were stuck and guided them to becoming unstuck, thus leaving them to draw energy, productivity, and abundance from their newly found Zentivity.

Zentivity worked for them! Try it for yourself—I'm sure you'll find it works for you too!

Follow Marianne on Social Media

Facebook.com/MarianneClydeLMFT
Twitter.com/marianneclyde
Pinterest.com/marianneclyde
YouTube.com/user/marianneclyde
www.marianneclyde.com
www.zentivity.guru

www.ingramcontent.com/pod-product-compliance
Lightning Source LLC
Chambersburg PA
CBHW030854180526
45163CB00004B/1565